Can We
Prayers of Love and Faith?

Mark Earey
Director of Anglican Formation and Tutor in Liturgy, The Queen's Foundation for Ecumenical Theological Education, Birmingham and Consultant Member of the Church of England Liturgical Commission

Phillip Tovey
Retired Principal, Oxford LMP
and former Warden of Readers

GROVE BOOKS LIMITED
RIDLEY HALL RD CAMBRIDGE CB3 9HU

Contents

1 Introduction 3

2 Understanding the Liturgical Package 5

3 Prayers for a Covenanted Friendship 12

4 The Resource Section 15

5 The Blessing of a Home 19

6 Beyond the Texts 25

Notes 27

Acknowledgments

The Group for Renewal of Worship thought long and hard about this booklet, conscious of the controversial nature of the liturgical material it tackles. Our aim as authors is not to take sides in an ongoing debate, and we are grateful for the support and encouragement of the Group in pursuing this approach.

The late Colin Buchanan had been due to write the booklet with us, and we acknowledge with thanks the early ideas that he contributed. We are particularly grateful to Andy Stinson and Patrick Angier for their contributions and comments on early drafts, and also to Liz Simpson and Amy Brown for their comments on later drafts of the booklet, which have helped to improve it further.

First Impression May 2024
ISSN 0144-1728
ISBN 978 1 78827 387 9

Introduction 1

The Prayers of Love and Faith (PLF) package has been some of the most controversial liturgical material to be produced in the Church of England for many years. This is partly because the content relates to the issue of same-sex relationships, which is proving to be an extremely divisive issue in the church, and partly because there is controversy even about the way the material has emerged and questions over the way it is being made available.

How the Material was Produced

PLF was not drafted by the Liturgical Commission but produced by the House of Bishops (primarily by the chair and vice-chair of the Commission, who are themselves bishops). It therefore appeared in a fairly final form (revised between the February and July General Synods in 2023, and further rearranged between then and the November 2023 Synod) without very much wider scrutiny or comment, beyond the seeking of feedback from Synod members after the February Synod. Presumably this approach was taken in order to keep control of, and responsibility for, the material in the hands of the House of Bishops.

It is not yet being seen as part of the *Common Worship* suite of resources, though this of itself is not without precedent (for instance, the 2020 book of resources about creation and the environment, *A Time for Creation,* exists alongside, rather than within, *Common Worship*). In many ways it shares commonalities with the *Common Worship* pastoral services volume, in that it includes material that is designed for more private and pastoral use as well as more public services.

The mechanisms by which the material has been made available have also been contested both in terms of their legality and their helpfulness, and the proposals have shifted and changed from one meeting of General Synod to the next. This of itself has been very confusing to many people.

The Approach of This Booklet

In all these controversies, the editorial group behind the Grove Worship series has reflected the range of views held in the wider church. Some of us feel comfortable using the full range of material; others are happy with some parts, but would not use others; others do not intend to use any of it.

This booklet, therefore, does not seek to take a line. Instead, it takes the material 'as is' without getting caught up in the ongoing debates about whether it should exist. We do not wish to downplay the importance of those debates, or to suggest that there is nothing more to be said. Rather, we seek to make a pragmatic contribution from a liturgical perspective: these texts do exist and have been made available for use in the Church of England (albeit with clear boundaries about how and when they can be used).

Our aim is to help people on all sides of the debate to see how PLF could be used, because some of the material is not, of itself, controversial (for example, the material for the blessing of a home). We also want to help those who will want to use the material more fully to do so well, within the constraints and processes that the House of Bishops have established.

The version of the material that we are working from is the document commended by the House of Bishops and published in December 2023 containing the following:[1]

- Prayers for a Covenanted Friendship
- The Resource Section
- The Blessing of a Home

Most of the booklet is focused on analyzing these resources and suggesting ways that they could be used. Chapter six looks beyond the texts themselves, recognizing that other aspects of how they are used will also be important, both with the texts we have and with any future standalone services.

However, because the process has been so confusing for many people, we begin in the next chapter with an explanation of what is in the package and how that has been shaped by the process. If you want to get straight to the practical material, feel free to jump straight to chapter three.

Pastoral Guidance

The liturgical material published in December 2023 came with a draft of the (partial) Pastoral Guidance document which had been presented to General Synod in November 2023.[2] This gives extensive guidance about how to discuss this material in local church contexts, how to make transparent decisions when there is disagreement (for instance, between an incumbent and a PCC) about whether the material should be offered in a local context (and which parts of it), and how to handle conflict. It also gives advice about meeting a couple and planning a service. This booklet, and the PLF material itself, should be read alongside that guidance.

Understanding the Liturgical Package

2

The motion passed by General Synod in November 2023 summarizes well the situation at that point:

> That this Synod, conscious that the Church is not of one mind on the issues raised by Living in Love and Faith, that we are in a period of uncertainty, and that many in the Church on all sides feel pain at this time, recognize the progress made by the House of Bishops towards implementing the motion on Living in Love and Faith passed by this Synod in February 2023, as reported in GS 2328, and encourage the House to continue its work of implementation, and ask the House to consider whether some standalone services for same-sex couples could be made available for use, possibly on a trial basis, on the timescale envisaged by the motion passed by the Synod in February 2023.

The Journey to the November 2023 Package

When the PLF material came to General Synod in February 2023, it consisted of one extended package of material that included what were referred to as 'sample services.' These sample services showed how to take resource material from the package and put it into a full service (one in the context of Holy Communion, and one as a Service of the Word).

At that point, the whole package was planned to be 'commended' by the House of Bishops for use under the minister's discretion within the provisions of Canon B5 (see below for more detail about the Canons and what they allow).[3]

PLF as presented at General Synod, February 2023

Prayers of Love and Faith
(including sample services)

Between the February and July Synod, the material underwent some revision, primarily to remove elements that some felt were 'too much like marriage.'[4]

In the report that was brought to the November 2023 General Synod (GS 2328), the House of Bishops had divided the package more clearly into three separate but connected parts:

- Prayers for a Covenanted Friendship—these are designed to mark a commitment between two persons which is explicitly *not* 'sexually intimate.' The couple are not necessarily of the same sex.
- Resources for use in private prayer with a same-sex couple, or for praying with them in the context of a church's regular worship (for example, as part of a main Sunday service)—in these resources, the degree of sexual intimacy of the couple is left unspoken, which means it is neither assumed nor denied.[5] This section included prayers for the blessing of a home.[6]
- Standalone services—that is, services in which the prayers for/blessing of the couple are the chief purpose of the service. These services were little different in content from the sample services provided previously.

PLF, as revised for General Synod, November 2023

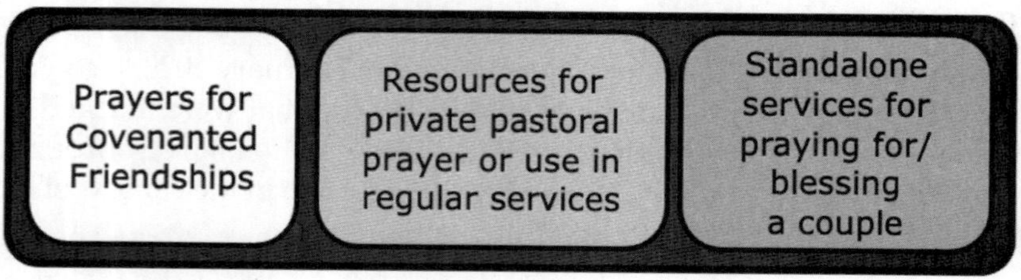

This division of the material made it easier to deal differently with each part, in response to the complex (and contested) arguments about *how* the material could be made legally available. To understand this, we need to understand the key canons under which the PLF might be made available:[7]

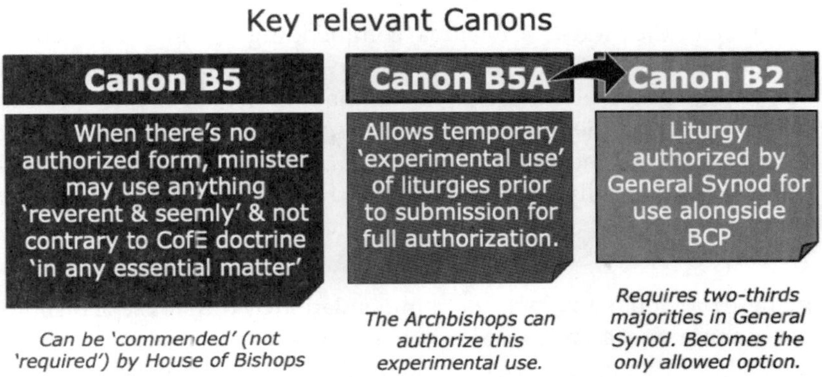

Canon B5

At the February General Synod, this was suggested as the Canon under which the whole package might be commended for use by the House of Bishops, without needing full synodical authorization.

Canon B5 gives permission to 'the minister' to provide their own material for situations where there is no provision in *The Book of Common Prayer* or in alternative authorized provision. This material must be 'reverent and seemly' and neither contrary to Church of England doctrine, nor 'indicative of any departure' from that doctrine 'in any essential matter.' Clearly, this has been a key area of controversy, as some in the church *do* see this as indicative of a change in the doctrine of marriage, whilst others maintain that it is not. This division is reflected in the House of Bishops itself, where different opinions are held, and votes have not been unanimous.

Because what is being provided is explicitly stated not to be a marriage, there is no material for this pastoral situation in the BCP. Hence, there is freedom for the minister to provide their own material. By commending the PLF the bishops would simply be saying that this material *is* 'reverent and seemly' and not contrary to CofE doctrine. They would be 'commending' this particular form, but without a requirement to use it or a restriction that this was the only appropriate form. In one sense, then, commendation is not providing anything new, in that this material (or something similar) could always have been used under the minister's discretion anyway. However, what it does make available is a set of centrally provided resources, allowing for a consistent offering across the church (rather than local invention), and a degree of reassurance that the material is appropriate to use for this purpose.

Where Does 'Commendation' Come From?

The idea of the House of Bishops 'commending' material covered by Canon B5 was originally intended to give a degree of authority and standing to relatively uncontroversial material which did not need to be authorized by General Synod because it did not have to be used. It was used, for instance, for material in *Lent, Holy Week, Easter* (1986) and (more controversially at the time) for the service of *Prayer and Dedication after Civil Marriage*, and it still covers much of the material in *Common Worship: Times and Seasons* (2006).

In these previous situations, the commendation by the House of Bishops was unanimous (as far as we know), so its use for material about which the bishops themselves are openly divided is a new departure.

Can You 'Un-commend' Liturgy?

Because liturgy commended by the House of Bishops is not required to be used by anyone, and because other suitable forms are still legitimate even when commended forms exist, in one sense there is no need to 'un-commend' anything, because it does not have to be used in the first place.

However, if further down the line, a differently configured House of Bishops felt that this material was not, after all, 'reverent and seemly', or that it was contrary to CofE doctrine in an essential matter, then they could, in theory, withdraw their commendation of that material. In practice, that might mean removing it from the CofE website. If it had made it into print, the situation might be more complicated.

No commended material has ever had its commendation withdrawn, but some commended material has quietly faded out of circulation. For instance, some of the commended seasonal material in earlier volumes such as *Promise of his Glory* or *Lent, Holy Week, Easter* did not make it into *Common Worship: Times and Seasons*. In this case it was not because there was any objection to the material—simply that there was not room for everything in the new single volume. The material remains commended and could still be used, it just is not explicitly part of *Common Worship*.

Canon B2

This is the canon under which liturgical material can be authorized by the General Synod. It has to be used for anything which is an alternative to something in the BCP, such as a service of Holy Communion, a set of collect prayers, or services of marriage, baptism or confirmation. Hence all the versions of those materials (and plenty of others) in *Common Worship* had to be authorized under Canon B2. It can also (but does not *have* to) be used for other material too—that is, new forms of worship which do not appear in the BCP.

Authorizing under Canon B2 involves going through the full synodical processes, including revision committees and votes in General Synod. To receive final approval, liturgical material has to receive two-thirds majorities in all three houses of General Synod (Bishops, Clergy and Laity).

Once a form of service is authorized in this way, it becomes (along with any pre-existing *Book of Common Prayer* version) the only form of service that can be used. This would enable the Synod to control the form of any service which was built primarily around the blessing of a same-sex couple.

This was originally going to be the proposal for the standalone services presented to the November 2023 General Synod, before the final motion was amended (see below).

Canon B5A

This is the canon under which services or liturgical material can be sent out for experimental use in parishes, prior to going through the full synodical process leading to full authorization under Canon B2 (described above). This is what the amendment proposed by the Bishop of Oxford introduced into the mix. This amendment forms the last part of the final motion approved by Synod in November 2023 (reproduced at the beginning of this chapter).

Are There Limits to Experimental Use?

When Canon B5A was used for trialling *Common Worship* services, the experimental use was for a limited time, and was also limited to a number of parishes in each diocese, nominated by the diocesan bishop. However, the text of the canon does not specify this, saying simply that the services can be trialled, 'for a period specified by them *[ie the archbishops]* on such terms and in such places or parishes as they may designate.'

The previous use of this canon assumed that the services being trialled were relatively uncontroversial versions of material within an existing category (such as a new funeral service or new eucharistic prayers). To use the canon to launch or test out a new category of liturgical rites is therefore unprecedented, even if lawful.

Different Texts—Different Canons

The separation of PLF into different sets of material allowed for the different parts of the package to be dealt with by different canonical provisions.

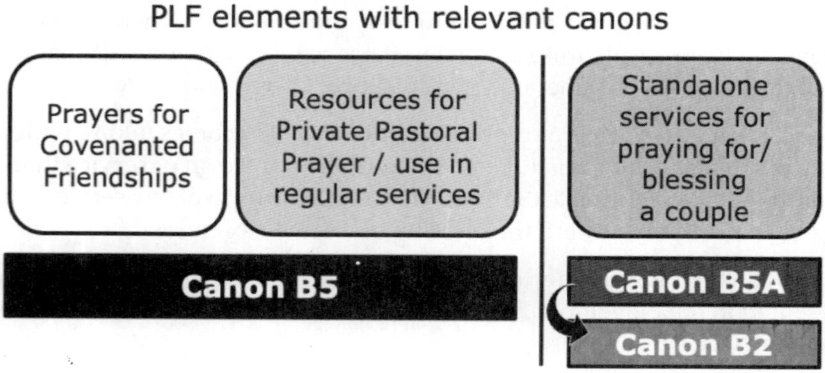

Following the November General Synod, the House of Bishops commended the *Prayers of Love and Faith* (now with the Blessing of a Home given a section of its own), together with *Pastoral Guidance*, on 12 December 2023, for use from Sunday 17 December within regular public worship or private prayer. It is this version which we have used for this booklet.

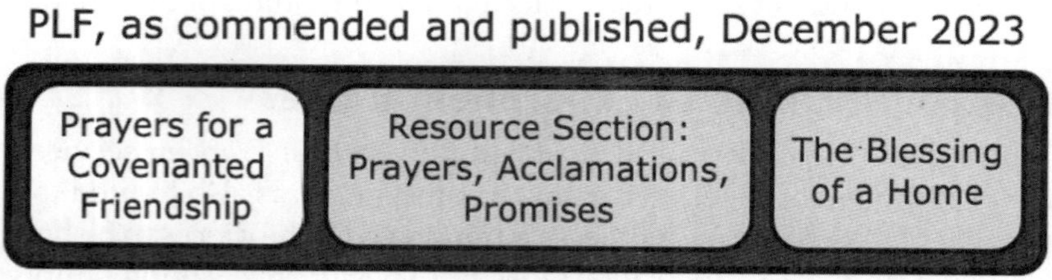

At the time of writing, the latest report to General Synod has spelt out in more detail the practical and pastoral issues raised by the idea of experimental use of standalone services (GS 2346, *Living in Love, Faith and Reconciliation*, February 2024).

It has also mentioned the possibility of using instead Canons B4.3 or 4.2, which allow for services to be authorized by, respectively, the archbishops (for use in their province, if allowed by diocesan bishops) or individual diocesan bishops. Under these canons, no synodical approval would be required, and no experimental use—they could be made available immediately. However, the report points out that this would introduce the risk of a postcode lottery about the availability of these services and produce a high risk of legal challenge. In the event, the report was brought to Synod, but a vote to 'Move to next business' meant that the debate ended without a vote on any formal motion to accept, take note of, or act on it.

When, how, and if standalone services will be made available remains, therefore, unclear at the time of writing. In the light of this, the rest of this booklet deals with the material which is currently available, and which was commended by the House of Bishops in December 2023.

3 Prayers for a Covenanted Friendship

This provision may come as a surprise to many, but is probably one of the least controversial parts of PLF. It consists of a short set of prayers for a committed but explicitly non-sexual relationship.[8] Though the covenanted friendship itself is not a sexual relationship, the parties are not (through these prayers) committing to celibacy—either or both of them could, for instance, be married to someone else. (If a calling to celibacy was discerned by either of the parties, then a commitment to the single consecrated life might be an appropriate route to consider.)

The material was included because it had been asked for in the Living in Love and Faith process. The idea is old and widespread. The ancient world had equivalents in *adelphopoiesis* (brother-making) and Christian liturgies for this are as old as marriage liturgies. Other cultures have ceremonies of blood-brotherhood. In popular culture, it is a part of the Shadowhunter world in the books and TV series, where each are called a *parabatai*. In all these contexts the commitment is to the platonic friendship and does not exclude the partners being married to others. David and Jonathan were seen to have such a relationship in the *Living in Love and Faith* materials.[9]

The Notes to the service give an explanation of the material and suggestions about the contexts in which it might be used, which include privately in church or a home, or as part of public worship.[10] In a more public setting it is suggested that Note 1 (which sets out the intention behind the prayers) be turned into a fuller introduction explaining the service.

There are three parts to the prayers.

- An introduction, addressed to the friends making the commitment. This could be supplemented as explained above by an introduction addressed to all those gathered.
- A prayer, spoken by the friends to one another, in which they commit themselves to support each other in love and friendship.
- A prayer 'for grace to dwell in the gift of devoted friendship,' said by the minister.

A Possible Scenario

St John's is a city-centre church with a teaching ministry that attracts students from the local university. They recently set up a pastoral group supporting those experiencing same-sex attraction who are committed to celibacy. The church took a strong role in the Living in Love and Faith process, contributing a perspective which sought to be faithful to what they saw as a traditional and biblical position on sexual relationships. The leadership and church council emphatically decided not to offer the general resources or proposed standalone services in PLF, although some in the pastoral group are exploring covenanted friendships. The Prayers for Covenanted Friendship could be used at the pastoral group in the prayer section of one of their regular meetings, for instance.

Elaine and Priti both experience same-sex attraction, but are committed to living within the church's traditional teaching and remaining celibate. They have been friends for several years, and have grown closer in friendship as they realized that they faced the same challenges. They find their friendship helps them maintain their commitment to celibacy, and now feel that they wish to mark the depth of their friendship and the support it brings with some prayers in church, supported by others in the pastoral group. They considered using the Covenanted Friendship material in the prayer section of one of the regular meetings of the pastoral group, but in the end asked the vicar to use some of the material in church on a Sunday morning, after the main service had finished. The vicar agreed, and several members of the pastoral support group stayed behind to join in.

Gathering

The vicar gave an extempore summary of Note 1 (PLF, p 2) to explain the service, followed by the opening address to Elaine and Priti (PLF, p 1 '*N* and *N*, we delight in your desire to dwell…')

Scripture

Romans 12.1, 2, 9–13 (PLF, p 18) was read and then the vicar shared some thoughts from the passage, as applied to this situation.

Commitment

Elaine and Priti used the commitment prayer ('I offer myself to you in love and friendship…' PLF, p 1)

Prayer

In a time of open prayer, some of the pastoral group prayed informally for Elaine and Priti.

The leader of the pastoral group said the Prayer for Companionship (PLF Resource section, p 8)

The vicar said the closing prayer from the Prayers for a Covenanted Friendship ('Faithful God…' PLF, p 1)

Everyone said The Grace together before they went to a local pub for lunch.

The Resource Section

4

A large part of PLF is the general resources section (pp 3–22). This is set out like *New Patterns for Worship* in various sections, designed to be used flexibly and incorporated as required into the other material in the package (Prayers for a Covenanted Friendship; Blessing of a Home; and any standalone services) or used in the context of more private pastoral prayers or in the context of regular public worship.

Comments on the Sections

Prayers of Gathering

Although the title suggests their use at the start of a service, the prayers 'For the Fruit of the Spirit' and 'For the Gift of Love' could be used at any point. The first prayer is simply the Prayer of Preparation from *Common Worship* Holy Communion. 'An Introductory Bidding' is not a prayer at all, but more like a statement of intent and an explanation of the prayers / service to follow.

Prayers of Dedication and Thanksgiving

There are five prayers in this section. The 'Prayer of Dedication' is not an act of dedication of the couple to each other, but a prayer for them to be enfolded in God's love and to follow the way of holiness.

The 'Prayer of Thanksgiving' and prayer 'For Guidance' are written as prayers spoken *by* the couple, whereas the prayers 'For Companionship' and 'For Grace to Live Well' are prayers *for* the couple (in which they can be named).

The section concludes with 'An Acclamation' (responsive in form) which could be led by the couple (which would make it feel more specific to their situation) or by a minister (which would make it feel more general). It could be used after a reading, at the end of a service, as the climax to some prayers.

Prayers for God's Blessing

There are three alternative prayers here, the last being the Aaronic blessing. The first two are carefully phrased as prayers for God's blessing ('By your blessing, may…'), rather than more declaratory blessings. In this they contrast sharply with the blessings in the marriage service (the bishops have been clear, as is PLF, that this is not a marriage).[11] The PLF prayers are for God to bless the couple, and thus are not 'gay marriage blessings' or 'same-sex relationship blessings.'

Prayers which May be Said with or by a Couple

This set of various prayers begins with the General Thanksgiving. Some are to be said by the minister, because they either name the couple directly or by implication ('you'). Some may be more appropriate for the couple to say (for instance, 'A prayer to the Holy Spirit,' PLF, p 11).

The prayer of commitment in the middle of the section is explicitly designed to be said by the couple. It is a prayer of dedication in a 'covenant of faith and hope.' It also envisages lifelong commitment, but does not include consent or vows as a marriage service would.

This section might have been clearer if the prayers a couple might say had been grouped together and distinguished more clearly from prayers for the couple by the minister.

Prayers for a Household and Family

There are five prayers in this section. Reference is made to the Blessing of a Home and the possibility therefore of these being used in that context. The prayers revolve around the theme of home and family and can include prayers for the couple's children. One is specifically named 'For a New Family Brought Together.' These prayers could clearly be pastorally appropriate and useful in many contexts, not just for a same-sex couple.

Psalms and Readings

Three psalms are suggested: 67, 121, 133.

Three passages from the Old Testament are included, David and Jonathan, Naomi and Ruth, and a passage from Jeremiah on the new covenant.

The six possible epistle readings are mostly exhortations to a life of Christian virtue.

Three gospel readings are given: the beatitudes and two from John's gospel ('I am the vine,' and 'abide in love'). These are only suggestions, so other passages could be read.

Summary

This is a set of pastoral prayers for a couple. It is only the context of the document which sets them in a same-sex context. They are clearly not a marriage, as there is no consent, or vows, or blessing of rings, or declaration of a new relationship. The prayer for God's blessing is a petition, not a declaratory blessing.

The Church of England, in these prayers, acknowledges the existence of different patterns of life and relationship and is willing to ask for God's blessing on the couple. This feels like a very small step to some, whilst being a step too far for others. Some scenarios, below, explore possible use of the prayers.

A Scenario—In the Setting of a Sunday Morning Service

St Matthew's is an inner-city church. They have been trying to reach out to those who go to clubs and those who walk the streets, mostly through a role as street pastors and opening a café in the building that provides cheap food, a warm place, and an open welcome. This has borne some fruit, and a same-sex couple recently joined the church. The church ran a few sessions on *Living in Love and Faith,* although study groups are not as central to church life as practical action expressing God's love. The minister and church council have decided to use the PLF if asked. They anticipate a couple coming forward for prayer after the intercessions, much like the prayers they already do for those who have birthdays and wedding anniversaries.

Billy and Chris recently joined the church. It began with a desire for a new life after working in the clubs. Billy had been helped one night by the street pastors after an altercation. They joined an enquirers' group and Chris got baptized. They have been together for 3 years, but knew one another from school. They wanted something very low key.

In the main Sunday service of Holy Communion, after the Intercessions and before the Peace, they came to the front and these prayers were used:

> A Prayer of Commitment by the Couple—PLF, p 12.
> A Prayer for God's Blessing—PLF, p 10 (second option)

The Peace was then said, and they were greeted by the congregation with applause. This is a very simple way to use the PLF resources.

A Scenario—In Choral Evensong

St Margaret's has a large choir. They have a BCP choral evensong at 3pm once a quarter, and there is usually a fairly large congregation. Alex and Jordan both sing in the choir and love choral evensong. They have been together for a long time and entered a civil partnership when the legislation was enacted. They asked 'to be blessed' in one of the services of choral evensong. After the collects, the vicar chose prayers from PLF, in consultation with the couple.

> An Introductory Bidding—PLF, p 6
> A Prayer of Dedication—PLF, p 7
> For Grace to Live Well—PLF, p 9

Prayers for God's Blessing—PLF, p 10 (first option)
For Support of Friends—PLF, p 14

The service then finished with a hymn (the choir doing a celebratory descant!) and a blessing. The readings and psalms were from the Resources section.

Conclusion

These scenarios demonstrate a simple way and a more complex way of using the prayers. In both cases these involve the adaptation of patterns of regular public worship that are already used. St Matthew's already had people come to the front before the peace for special prayers. Evensong has long allowed for extra material to be added at the end (not least, a sermon). In this case some PLF resources were part of those additions.[12] This context enabled a fuller provision.

5

The Blessing of a Home

The prayer for the blessing of a home is a welcome part of PLF. There has been no previous official liturgical provision for blessing a home in the Church of England, though in practice it happens a lot and there have been plenty of unofficial liturgies and resources to support it.[13]

The Blessing of a Home in PLF is taken from the recently commended *Liturgical Resources for the Ministry of Deliverance* (2023).[14] The blessing of a home might be an appropriate part of the response to a range of pastoral situations: deliverance; moving into a new home; or as suggested here, linked to PLF. Some couples might want to make their home the location of prayers for blessing and see this as a celebration to be shared with friends and family.

Structure

The material is set out in the following sections, assuming this structure for a service (PLF, pp 26ff).

The Gathering
- At the Entrance
- On the Land

Entry
- At the Main Door

In the Home
- In Bedrooms
- In a Study or Workroom
- In the Kitchen
- At a Table
- In the Living Room

Prayers
- The Lord's Prayer

The Conclusion

An outline structure is also provided, which assumes a service including Holy Communion (PLF, p 25), and there are notes and propers for Holy Communion at the end of the material (PLF, pp 32–35). Oddly, there is no outline structure for a service without Holy Communion, so it is not made clear that a reading (or readings) from the Bible should be included in such services. If planning such a service, it is probably best to use and adapt the outline structure from PLF, p 25 as the basis for the service.

The first thing to say about this order is that it is only proposed and can be reordered to fit the circumstances. There are suggestions about the entirely optional use of water, oil and the sign of the cross in a set of general notes at the beginning (PLF, pp 23–24). Often in such blessings, candles have been lit in various rooms, so there is plenty to think about and plan. Keeping to a few simple but memorable actions is probably better than overloading the service.

In addition, it would be entirely possible to substitute some of the house blessing prayers with Resource Section prayers if the home blessing was the context for prayers or a blessing for a couple themselves too. If this were the case, it would be important to do the act of commitment early in the service, as it confirms the relationship, and to leave the prayers for God's blessing on the couple towards the end as the climax of the service. You would need to think through how this would flow and how much you could move round depending on the size of the home and the number of people present.

There is a great opportunity to include children, and the prayers also offer time for the couple to pray together. Access will be an issue for some people and that also needs to be considered. Ways of doing this are suggested in the following worked examples.

A Scenario—Praying for a Home and Family

St Anne's is in a seaside town, once a fishing village, but now mostly involved in day tourism in the summer, though there are also several hotels and B&B businesses. St Anne's was marginally involved in LLF, a small group going to a diocesan event. However, the Reader was a LLF advocate, and the vicar and PCC have been happy to begin experimenting with using parts of PLF.

Simon and Jack run a hotel in the town. They have been together for 15 years, had a civil marriage ceremony, and have adopted two children, aged 12 and 10 respectively. They live in a house next to the hotel and Simon is the churchwarden and Jack the organist. They asked for the blessing of their home, including the family. One of the grandparents has mobility issues and a large chair was reserved for them to use on the ground floor. 20–25 guests came, and the function room in the hotel was used for a celebration meal afterwards. The service was led by the Reader, as follows:

Entry

The Prayer At the Main Door (PLF, p 27) was used at the front door of the house, with the congregation gathering (carefully!) on the pavement. One of the guests was video-calling the proceedings to the grandparent with limited mobility, who was already installed in their chair in the living room.

In the Home

Prayers were said in bedrooms and the kitchen, at the dining table and in the living room (PLF, pp 28–29).

The Liturgy of the Word

Everyone squeezed into the living room for the Bible reading, done by one of the children: Eph 3.14-end, as in PLF, p 19.

Prayers

The other churchwarden led the Prayer For a Home (PLF, p 15). Everyone gathered in a circle, with the couple and their children in the centre, and everyone stretched out a hand towards them as the Reader led the Prayer for God's Blessing—PLF Resource section, p 10 (second prayer) and A Prayer for a Couple's Family—PLF Resource section, p 16.

The Reader led everyone in The Lord's Prayer

The Conclusion

Led by the Reader, with a shouted 'Amen' at the end (PLF, p 31).

This order simplified the home blessing, but kept its structure. The Bible passage was one of the suggested readings, which mentions families. At each of the stations a candle was lit by one of the children. Three prayers were taken from the Resource Section. It was important to choose prayers that did not suggest a new family, but rather prayed for God's blessing for something that was already in existence.

Although the scenario envisages a same-sex couple, something similar could be used (for instance) by a heterosexual couple whose recent marriage has brought together children from the couple's previous relationships, and who want to ask for God's blessing on a new home and family formed by their marriage.

A Scenario including Holy Communion

St Mary's is a charismatic church. They have been heavily involved with the diocesan schools department in setting up a Church of England Academy in the new housing area. They have already done several baptisms for children of same-sex couples, and some now come regularly to the church. The school involvement has put them in the middle of gender identity questions, and they used Living in Love and Faith as a springboard to study both the Bible and contemporary questions of sexuality. Some members of the youth group use non-binary pronouns. There is a variety of opinion in the church, but they want to try to live out a reconciled diversity in love. They have agreed to use PLF particularly in the blessing of a home. The prayers would be selected for the situation of each couple.

Sue and Ella had their child baptized at St Mary's and now are regulars. They wanted their relationship and home 'blessed by the church' and invited 30 church friends to come along to the celebration, which included a barbeque in the garden. They wanted to include Holy Communion, and the informal service ended up looking like this:

The Gathering

Informal welcome with songs, in the back garden
Prayers of Penitence—PLF, p 33
The Collect—PLF, p 33

Home Blessing

Prayers were said in the bedrooms, Sue's home office, the kitchen and the living room—drawn from PLF, pp 28–29
Everyone, gathered in the kitchen-diner, joined in a time of open praise.

The Liturgy of the Word

Ruth 1.15–22 and John 20.19–23—as suggested in the PLF Resource and Home Blessing sections respectively
Short talk—given by their home group leader
Words of knowledge and prophecy

Prayers

The vicar laid hands on the couple and said A Prayer of Dedication (PLF, p 7) and a Prayer of Blessing (PLF, p 10, first prayer)
Others then led A Prayer for a Couple's Family—PLF, p 16 and A Prayer as a Couple Make a Home Together—PLF, p 16
A time of open prayer followed, in which others prayed for the couple and their home

The Liturgy of the Sacrament

The Peace was shared informally.
The Eucharistic Prayer included a proper preface from PLF p 34.
The Lord's Prayer was said.
Breaking of the Bread (which had been baked by the couple).
Giving of Communion, in which people passed the bread and wine to each other.

Prayer after Communion.

The Conclusion

Post Communion prayer—PLF, p 34.

Prayer for God's blessing on the couple—PLF, p 10.

The Blessing

By adding Holy Communion this was necessarily a longer service. Communion was celebrated on the main kitchen table with folk sitting and standing around. Spaces for the exercise of spiritual gifts and song were provided, and the whole service had an informal, joyful style and pastoral warmth about it. The service included a mixture of prayers from the Blessing a Home section and Resource section.

A Scenario Incorporating Prayers for a Covenanted Friendship

St Peter's is a village church that thinks of itself as 'middle of the road.' The village is near to a town with many retired people and commuters. It wants to keep the village community alive and be open to all comers. Cassius and Ryan, committed Christians, already live together in a platonic relationship and are moving into the village. Their close friends at the church wanted to throw a housewarming party, and so the minister offered to come and do some simple prayers at their new flat at the start of the party. Here is what they came up with, using a simplified version of the house blessing as a structure.

Entry

At the Main Door (PLF, p 27) was used at the door to the flat, with everyone gathered on the landing outside (neighbours had been invited to join in).

In the Home

In the Living Room—PLF, p 29.

The Liturgy of the Word

Reading: 1 Sam 18.1–5 (David and Jonathan)—as suggested in PLF Resource section, p 17.

A short talk by the minister.

Prayers

Prayers for A Covenanted Friendship—drawn from PLF, p 1.

Informal prayers led by some of their friends.

The Lord's Prayer.

The Conclusion

Aaronic blessing—PLF, p 11.

The service was kept simple, with elements of the word and free prayer. The reading was chosen as a biblical example of a covenanted friendship. This commitment has no legal implications, so if Cassius and Ryan are buying the property together, then legal arrangements would have to be made separately.

Conclusion

There are many possibilities of combining prayers from The Resource Section with the Blessing of a Home. The individual situation of the couple needs to be considered and they may wish to be involved in the design of the service. In all the cases a party is included, but this is not essential. It is probably good practice to record the Home Blessing in the register of services (not the marriage register) in church.

6

Beyond the Texts

Part of the challenge of the PLF material, from the very beginning, has been the tension between a desire on the part of some for these services to 'do' something (or else why bother?) and the view of others that they must not do something that suggests we have changed our doctrine of marriage (that is, any services or elements within them, must not look like a wedding).

In practice, holding this tension will be as much about how the prayers are said, the context in which they take place, and the actions that accompany them, as it will be about the words of the prayers themselves.[15] This might include things such as:

- How the couple are dressed.[16]
- How they arrive at the service (any separate arrivals start to look like a traditional wedding service).
- What actions the minister performs (for instance, any stole-wrapping around joined hands would look like a wedding).
- What actions the couple perform (exchanging rings, for instance, would be ruled out).
- Any provision of a certificate (the Pastoral Guidance suggests a 'keepsake card' might be appropriate).[17]

How Would a Standalone Service be Different?

One of the (many) confusions around the PLF material is working out why resources for use in a regular service can be commended for use under the minister's discretion, but standalone services (which are based on the same resources) need a different treatment. How is a standalone service different from any other service in which material from the PLF resource section is used? The answer probably relates to the 'extra-textual' matters noted above, as well as how the service is described and enacted, and what 'title' it is given.

Perhaps by separating out the standalone services from the other material, the bishops were recognizing that this wider *context* in which the material is used will be key in interpreting what is being offered. A standalone service is one which is only taking place because of the relationship being marked—that is, it is an 'occasional office' in the technical sense of a service 'occasioned by' this pastoral situation, rather than a service that is taking place anyway, in which this pastoral need happens to be being acknowledged as part of something else. It therefore starts to look more like a rite of passage in a similar category to a baptism, a funeral or a wedding. This is what would make such a standalone service more likely to be interpreted as a same-sex wedding—the very thing that the bishops insist is not happening.

PLF as Pastoral Services

Ministers who are leading services in which same-sex couples are being prayed with and/or blessed, will need to be aware of this wider context and skilful in making the service do enough to function as a service that cares for the people involved, without doing so much that it pushes beyond what the Church of England has currently committed itself to.

It can help to be aware of the key principles that apply to all acts of worship that respond to pastoral needs. In general, any pastoral service will need three key things:[18]

- A human story—that is, an articulation of the pastoral need being addressed (for example, in a funeral, a telling of the story of the person who has died).
- A God story—that is, an articulation of where God is in this story (for example, in a funeral, the Christian understanding of the death and resurrection of Christ, and its implications for us).
- A liminal moment—that is, a point of transition, the moment when the service 'does something.'

In relation to prayers and blessings for same-sex couples, all three are complex and in different ways contested. The human story is perhaps the most straightforward, in that it addresses the reality which this pastoral response is addressing. The God story is more contested, because this is where the division in the Church of England manifests itself: is the God story that God delights in this relationship or that God delights in the persons but considers the form of the relationship to be sinful?

In particular, there is a challenge about what the transition is. The House of Bishops have been clear that the transition is not the same as a wedding—the couple are not moving from'not married' to 'married,' and the legal status of their relationship is not changed in any way.[19]

It is not even clear that the *relationship* itself is moving from 'not blessed' to 'blessed'—rather, the liturgical material focuses on the *persons,* and prays for God's blessing for them. What the liturgical material might do is mark the couple moving from a position in which their relationship is not officially recognized by the church at all, to a position in which it is acknowledged, and in which they (though not necessarily the relationship itself) can be prayed for, for God's blessing on all that is good about the relationship. The job of the minister working with the couple is to put this in liturgical form.

The biggest risk with any pastoral service is that it becomes a service themed around the pastoral situation, rather than a service that does something in response to that situation. Pastoral services need a ritual liminal moment. This can be signalled simply. For instance: a prayer with laying on of hands; a change of posture by the whole congregation such as all standing; the offering of applause. Whilst being aware of the issues outlined above at the start of this chapter, any use of the PLF material will need to make sure that the journey from human story to God story to response is concluded with some action and/or symbol (as well as the words), which will signal that the prayers or service have done their job.

All of this must be taken into account in the use of the commended material already available, but it will particularly come into focus if and when any standalone services are provided.

Notes

1 House of Bishops, *Prayers of Love and Faith* (December 2023)

2 House of Bishops, *Living in Love and Faith: Pastoral Guidance* (Version 1, December 2023)

3 The final resolution from the February 2023 General Synod included: 'This Synod...(e) welcome the response from the College of Bishops and look forward to the House of Bishops further refining, commending and issuing the Prayers of Love and Faith described in GS 2289 and its Annexes; (f) invite the House of Bishops to monitor the Church's use of and response to the Prayers of Love and Faith, once they have been commended and published, and to report back to Synod in five years' time; (g) endorse the decision of the College and House of Bishops not to propose any change to the doctrine of marriage, and their intention that the final version of the Prayers of Love and Faith should not be contrary to or indicative of a departure from the doctrine of the Church of England.'

4 GS 2303, 'Update to General Synod of the Implementation Work for Living in Love and Faith', July 2023, para 9: '...at the February Synod there was the opportunity to submit written comments on the Prayers of Love and Faith...Overall the most significant critical comments were that the PLF were too much like marriage (60 responses); they don't go far enough (44 responses); and that more pastoral guidance would be required for their use (42 responses). Other ideas were also

presented, ranging from specific textual suggestions to more general observations.'.

5 This is explicitly stated in the Pastoral Guidance published in December 2023 ('The PLF make no assumptions with regards to sexual intimacy...') p 16, section 1.2.3.

6 The actual material was not printed in GS 2328, but a note said, '[Insert here the rite for the Blessing of a Home in the form commended by the House of Bishops in July 2023.]. This form was commended as part of material for deliverance ministry, which was made available on the CofE website (search for 'Liturgical Resources for Mental Health and Wellbeing' and scroll down to the 'Liturgical Resources for the Ministry of Deliverance'). The full text was included in the version of PLF published in December 2023.

7 For more detail about the difference between authorized and commended material, and how this connects to the Canons of the Church of England, see Mark Earey, *Finding Your Way Around Common Worship* (London: CHP, 2011) pp 14–16.

8 There is more explanation of the idea of Covenanted Friendship as it is used in PLF in the Pastoral Guidance published in December 2023, pp 18–19.

9 Archbishops' Council, *Living in Love and Faith* (London: CHP, 2020) pp 180–181.

10 PLF, p 2.

11 They also contrast with the Church in Wales, where there are services for blessing after a civil same-sex marriage in which the couple are blessed directly (God the Father...bless you) and the minister may wrap a stole around the couple's hands. Church in Wales, *Liturgy for the Blessing of a Same-sex Civil Marriage or Civil Partnership* (October 2021). This is authorized for experimental use for 5 years, where the diocesan bishop has allowed its use.

12 This case is specifically mentioned in PLF, p 5.

13 See, for instance, John Leach and Liz Simpson, *Bless this House* (Grove Worship booklet S204); David Silk (comp), *Prayers to Use at the Alternative Services* (London: Mowbray, 1980) and Richard Deadman *et al* (eds), *Pastoral Prayers: A Resource for Pastoral Occasions* (London Mowbray, 1996) pp 5–9.

14 These can be found on the Church of England website, in the section of 'Liturgical Resources for Mental Health and Wellbeing.'

15 This is specifically addressed in the Pastoral Guidance, pp 22–23.

16 See Pastoral Guidance, p 23, section 1.3.6.

17 'Churches can design a keepsake card if they wish to do so in order to mark the occasion. This would be purely commemorative and have no official or legal status. Such certificates must not suggest or imply in their wording or design that they commemorate or are proof of a marriage.' Pastoral Guidance, p 22, section 1.3.4.

18 For more about the principles of pastoral services in general, see Mark Earey, *Worship That Cares: An Introduction to Pastoral Liturgy* (London: SCM Press, 2012), especially chapters 2 and 3.

19 See, for instance, Pastoral Guidance, p 24, section 1.3.8.